Food for (

See Your Child Grow Up Well!

Healthy & Delicious
Food for Children
See Your Child Grow Up Well!

Anuradha Sinha

Nita Mehta
PUBLICATIONS

Healthy & Delicious
Food for Children

© Copyright 2000-2006 *Nita Mehta* PUBLICATIONS

5th Print 2006
ISBN 81-7676-005-6

Food Styling and Photography: *Nita Mehta* PUBLICATIONS

Layout and laser typesetting :

National Information Technology Academy
3A/3, Asaf Ali Road
New Delhi-110002
☎ 23252948

Published by :

Nita Mehta
PUBLICATIONS
3A/3 Asaf Ali Road, New Delhi-110002
Tel: 91-11-23250091, 29214011, 23252948, 29218727
Fax: 91-11-29225218, 91-11-23250091
E-Mail : nitamehta@email.com
Website : http://www.nitamehta.com, http://www.snabindia.com

Distributed by :

THE VARIETY BOOK DEPOT
A.V.G. Bhavan, M 3 Con Circus,
New Delhi - 110 001
Tel : 23417175, 23412567; Fax : 23415335
Email: varietybookdepot@rediffmail.com

Printed by :
PRESSTECH LITHO PVT LTD, NEW DELHI

Rs. 89/-

Foreword

"My child does not eat anything!" What to do? This is the common problem faced by mothers of growing children. *Healthy & Delicious* **Food for Children** has been written to solve this dilemma of young mothers.

The author of the book is a mother of two healthy children. She is also a school teacher and has a long association with children as well as their parents. Their needs, likes and dislikes are very well known to her.

Each recipe in this book has been tried several times and does not need any elaborate cooking. All the ingredients used are easily available in every kitchen. Apart from being easy-to-cook and good to eat, they are all very nutritive and healthy.

A balanced diet consists of different types of food in the right quantity. To increase the nutritive content of foods, soya bean powder made by grinding soya nutrinuggets, has been added. It enhances the food's nutrition without disturbing the taste. Ground almonds & peanuts too are added in many recipes to fulfil the extra protein needs of a growing child. Now relax and watch your child grow up well!

Nita Mehta

USEFUL TIPS

♦ Some recipes require almond powder and soya bean powder. It is very handy if you make them into a powder and store them separately in air tight bottles (soyabean powder can be obtained by grinding the soya nutrinuggets).

♦ Palak paste can be made by blanching washed palak leaves and making a puree in the mixer. This can be kept covered in a container and refrigerated. This remains good for a week. It can be used in various recipes and saves a lot of time.

♦ Always keep boiled potato, unpeeled in the refrigerator. They come handy when needed.

♦ Dalia can be roasted in a large quantity and kept in an air tight container.

♦ Roasted dalia could be boiled once for about 3-4 days and kept in the refrigerator. When required it could just be boiled with milk for sweet dalia and used otherwise for upma.

Contents

Tiffin Box

It is so delightful for a mother to see that her child has eaten his food in school. But most mothers feel that their children are not eating their tiffin at school. They actually want variety in their food. From the recipes under this heading, you could easily choose something interesting and different to give your child, each day of the week.

In the morning one is always short of time. Something special for the tiffin seems impossible. But it is not so, if planned properly on the previous night. The final cooking and the packing could be left for the morning. The packing of the food in the lunch box should also appeal to the child just as much as its taste.

Nutritive Maggie Hearts

Picture on cover
Serves 4

1 packet maggie masala noodles - boiled till just done
1 carrot - grated (3/4 cup)
3/4 cup finely chopped cabbage
2 tbsp atta (whole wheat flour)
2 tbsp butter
¾ cup milk
3/4 tsp salt, or to taste
1 tbsp almond powder (8-10 almonds ground)
1 tbsp nutrinugget powder
salt and pepper to taste

1. Boil maggie noodles in just 1 cup water on medium flame till the water gets absorbed.
2. Melt butter in a heavy bottomed kadhai on low heat.
3. Add atta and stir fry for 1 minute. Add milk stirring continuously.
4. Add carrots, cabbage, nutrinugget powder, almond powder and cook till thick. Add salt.
5. Add boiled maggie. Cook for 2-3 minutes more and keep mixing the noodles gently till the mixture turns really thick. Do not mash the noodles.
6. Cook till the mixture turns thick enough to be shaped into cutlets. Remove from fire. Cool.
7. With oiled hands, make heart shaped cutlets and refrigerate overnight. Next morning shallow or deep fry them.

Note: *You may grind the almonds and the nutrinuggets together in a small coffee or spice grinder and store in an air tight bottle.*

GOLD COINS

Serves 4-5

6 bread slices
2 small potatoes - boiled
1 small onion - chopped finely
1 carrot - chopped finely
1 capsicum - chopped finely
¼ cup finely chopped cabbage
¼ tsp haldi
½ tsp pepper, ¼ tsp amchoor, ½ tsp garam masala
salt to taste
¼ cup maida dissolved in ¼ cup water
bread crumbs
oil for frying

1. Grate boiled potatoes.
2. Heat 1½ tbsp oil. Add onions. Cook till transparent.
3. Add cabbage, carrot and capsicum. Cook for 3-4 minutes on low flame.
4. Add potatoes, haldi, salt, pepper, amchoor and garam masala. Cook for 2-3 minutes. Keep aside.
5. With a cutter or a sharp lid of a bottle, cut out small rounds (about 1½" - 2" diameter) of the bread, 2 rounds from each slice.
6. Spread some potato mixture on the round piece of bread. Press.
7. Spread maida paste over the potato mixture.
8. Sprinkle bread crumbs. Press.
9. Deep fry in hot oil. Dot with tomato ketchup.

Soya~Palak Puri

Serves 4

1 cup atta (wheat flour), approx.
¼ cup soya powder made by grinding nutrinuggets
1 tbsp suji
1 cup palak (spinach) - chopped
½ tsp salt

1. Put the palak leaves with ¼ cup water to boil. Boil for 2 minutes. Cool.
2. Blend in a mixer to a puree.
3. Mix all ingredients with the palak puree and make a dough, without adding water. Keep covered for 10-15 minutes.
4. Heat oil in a kadhai. Make small puries and fry in oil. Serve with tomato ketchup.

Note: *Boil beetroot or pumpkin and blend to a puree. Use in place of palak to get lovely red or yellow puries.*

MANGO PANCAKE

Serves 4

1 ripe mango - chopped
¾ cup atta (whole wheat flour)
¾ cup milk, approx.
oil for frying

1. Put chopped mango, atta and milk in a mixer and blend to a smooth, thin batter
2. Heat a pan. Add a tsp of oil in the pan and spread it.
3. Add 2 tbsp of the pancake batter and spread it like a dosa. Put 1 tsp of oil around it and reduce flame. Cover the pan with a lid. Leave for 2 minutes.
4. Uncover, increase flame, put ½ tsp oil over the pancake and turn it. Let it cook for 1 minute. Take it out on a plate & serve hot:

VEGETABLE PANCAKES

Picture on facing page
Serves 6

¾ cup suji (semolina)
¼ cup atta (whole wheat flour)
½ cup curd
1½ cups water
½ tsp salt, ¼ tsp eno (fruit salt)

FILLING

3/4 cup finely chopped cabbage
1 small carrot - cut into match sticks (3/4 cup)
2 tbsp finely chopped green coriander
1 medium onion - finely chopped
1 tsp ginger - finely chopped
1 medium tomato - chopped
2 cubes cheese - grated (¼ cup)
salt, pepper to taste

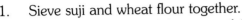

1. Sieve suji and wheat flour together.
2. Add curd and water. Make a smooth batter of a thin pouring consistency.
3. Allow the batter to stand for 30 minutes.
4. To prepare the filling, heat oil in a kadhai. Add chopped onions and ginger. Reduce flame. Bhuno on medium flame till soft. Add tomatoes. Bhuno for 2 minutes, add carrot and cabbage. Bhuno for 2 minutes. Remove from fire. Add the grated cheese, coriander, salt and pepper. Mix well. Keep filling aside.
5. To prepare the pancakes, beat the batter. Add eno and mix well.
6. Spread ½ tsp of oil or butter on a non stick pan.
7. Put a karchhi of batter onto the hot pan and spread evenly all over the bottom of the pan.
8. Cook quickly on one side until golden brown.
9. Turn and cook on the other side.
10. Put some filling and roll it up. Serve hot.

Soya~Aloo ki Puri

Serves 4

1 cup atta (wheat flour)
¼ cup soya powder made by grinding nutrinuggets
1 tbsp suji
3 medium potatoes - boiled & mashed
¼ tsp salt
¼ tsp jeera powder (optional)

1. Mix all ingredients and make a dough without adding water to it. If required add very little water.
2. Keep covered for 10-15 minutes.
3. Heat oil in a kadhai. Make puries with the dough and fry in oil.

Note: *This dough should not be kept out for a longer time. However, it can be kept in the refrigerator for more than 24 hours.*

Moong Sprout Parantha

Serves 4

STUFFING

1 cup saboot moong dal or ready-made fresh moong sprouts
1 small onion - finely chopped
1" piece ginger - finely chopped
2 flakes garlic - finely chopped
a pinch of hing
oil
salt to taste

DOUGH

1 cup wheat flour
1 tbsp soya powder - made by grinding nutrinuggets

1. Soak saboot moong overnight in 2 cups water in a warm place. Cover it with a net.
2. On the next day in the evening, you will find small white sprouts coming out of it. (You may use fresh moong sprouts available with vegetable vendors.)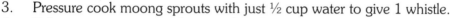
3. Pressure cook moong sprouts with just ½ cup water to give 1 whistle.
4. If there is excess water, dry it on fire. Remove from fire and cool.
5. Heat 2 tsp oil. Add hing and the chopped onion, ginger & garlic. When the onions turn transparent, add the boiled moong sprouts and salt. Mix it well and mash moong well.
6. Make a chappati dough with wheat flour, soya powder & water.
7. Make stuffed paranthas with the above moong filling and fry on tawa with ghee on oil.

SPECIAL FULL MEAL DOSA

Serves 4-5

1 tbsp Channa dal
1 tbsp dhuli Moong dal
1 tbsp saboot Moong
1 tbsp Urad dal
1 tbsp saboot Masoor
1 tbsp rice
1½ tbsp nutrinugget powder - made by grinding nutrinuggets
1 tbsp coriander chopped
1 tsp ginger - finely chopped
salt to taste
oil

1. Soak together all the dals & rice in 3 cups of water, for 4-5 hours.
2. Grind the above in a mixer to obtain the consistency of dosa batter.
3. Add chopped coriander, finely chopped ginger and nutrinugget powder and salt.
4. Heat a tawa and put a tsp of oil. Sprinkle water and wipe it. With a ½ cut potato, wipe the tawa.
5. Pour 2 tbsp of the batter and spread it like a dosa and pour oil on its sides. Let it cook on both sides.
6. Serve with tomato sauce.

MOONG SPROUT APPLE BURGER

Picture on page 1
Makes 6

6 small burger buns
butter enough to spread
2 cubes cheese - grated
1 apple - cut into slices, juice of ½ lemon

TIKKI
2 boiled potatoes - mashed or grated
½ cup moong sprouts
1 tbsp butter
1 onion - finely chopped
1 tbsp tomato ketchup
1 tsp salt, or to taste
¼ tsp amchoor, ½ tsp bhuna jeera powder, ½ tsp garam masala
1 slice of bread - dipped in water and squeezed well

1. Wash moong sprouts and pressure cook with ¼ cup of water and ¼ tsp of salt to give one whistle. Remove from fire and keep aside.
2. Heat 1 tbsp butter and fry onions till light pink.
3. Add the steamed sprouts and stir fry for a minute. Remove from fire.
4. Add the mashed potatoes, tomato ketchup, grated cheese, bhuna jeera powder, garam masala, amchoor and salt to taste. Mix well.
5. Make small tikkis, according to the size of buns and keep in the refrigerator at night.
6. Next morning fry the tikkis in a pan in some oil and keep aside.
7. Cut the buns into half. Spread butter generously on both pieces and press on a hot tawa to make them light brown.
8. Put a tikki on the bun.
9. Cut an apple into round slices and sprinkle some lemon juice on them. Put a round slice of apple on the bun.
10. Fold the already folded napkin into a triangle and wrap half of the bun in the napkin. Keep it neatly in the tiffin.

Note: *You may microwave the sprouts with a sprinkling of water in a plastic bag for 2 minutes, instead of using the pressure cooker.*

KATHI NUGGET ROLLS

Picture on facing page

Serves 4

COVERING DOUGH
1 cup maida, 1 cup atta
½ tsp salt

MARINATE TOGETHER
1 cup soya nuggets - soaked in warm water for ½ hour, drained & squeezed
1½ tsp ginger-garlic paste
1 tbsp cornflour
½ tsp salt

OTHER INGREDIENTS FOR THE FILLING
3 tbsp oil
½ tsp ajwain
2 onions - cut into 4 pieces

2 firm tomatoes - cut into 4 pieces
½ tsp soya sauce
½ tbsp tomato sauce
½ tsp vinegar
salt and pepper to taste

1. Soak the nuggets in warm water for half an hour. Squeeze out and wash thoroughly in 3-4 changes of cold water.
2. Marinate the nuggets with cornflour, salt and ginger-garlic paste. Leave it aside for 15 minutes.
3. Knead the maida & atta with salt, into a smooth dough. Cover and keep the dough aside till the filling is ready.
4. To prepare the filling, cut the onions into 4 large pieces and separate the layers. Chop the tomatoes also into 4 pieces and remove the pulp.
5. Heat 2 tbsp oil. Add the marinated soya nuggets to it and keep frying for 5-7 minutes or till slightly brown. Remove from the kadhai.
6. Heat 1 tbsp of oil in the same kadhai, add the ajwain and the onion. Fry on high flame for 3 minutes.

7. Add the tomatoes and fry for another 2 minutes.
8. Add the fried soya nuggets, mix well for 2 minutes.
9. Add both the sauces, vinegar, a pinch of salt and a pinch of pepper. Mix thoroughly for 2 more minutes. Remove from fire.
10. Make round paranthas with the prepared dough and spread a row of the nugget filling and roll it up.
11. Wrap it in a paper napkin at one end and serve.

CHANNA DAL PARANTHA

Serves 4

wheat flour (atta) dough for paranthas
1½ cups channa dal - washed & soaked in 2½ cups warm water for 2-3 hours
1 tbsp oil
a pinch of hing
¼ tsp ajwain
2 flakes garlic - crushed
½ inch ginger - finely chopped
salt to taste

1. Pressure cook channa dal in the same water in which it is soaked for 15 minutes on medium heat after the first whistle.
2. Heat 1 tbsp oil in the kadhai, add hing, ajwain, ginger and garlic. Fry for a few seconds. Add the boiled channa dal alongwith the water and fry till the water completely evaporates. Add salt and mix well. Let it cook till the dal turns absolutely dry.
3. Using the wheat flour dough, make paranthas with this dal stuffing.
4. Spread sauce or chutney on the parantha, roll it up in aluminium foil or paper napkin in the tiffin.

SALTY PANCAKES

Serves 4

½ cup maida (plain flour)
½ cup besan (gram flour)
1 tbsp suji (semolina)
½ tsp Eno fruit salt
¼ tsp salt or to taste
¾ cup mixture of finely minced or grated cabbage, onion, ginger, carrot &
finely chopped coriander
oil for frying

1. Mix all the ingredients with 1½ cups water. Mix well. Add more water if required to get a batter of a pouring consistency.
2. Heat a pan on medium flame. Add 1 tsp oil and spread 2 tbsp batter in it. Put oil on the sides. Cover & cook on low flame for 2 minutes.
3. Uncover. Put 1 tsp oil over it and turn it. Cook on medium flame for 2 minutes.
4. Spread some sauce on the pancake and roll it up.
5. Wrap in aluminium foil.

BANANA PANCAKES

Serves 4

2 bananas - mashed
¼ cup atta (wheat flour), ½ cup maida (plain flour)
1¼ cups milk, ½ tsp vanilla essence
oil for frying

1. Slice bananas and grind in mixer with ½ cup milk.
2. Add maida, wheat flour, vanilla eseence and the remaining milk to the mixer. Beat all the ingredients together till a smooth batter is obtained.
3. Heat a pan on fire. Add a tsp of oil in the pan and spread it.
4. Add 2 tbsp of the pancake batter and spread it like a dosa. Put 1 tsp of oil around it and reduce flame. Cover the pan with a lid. Leave for 2 minutes.
5. Uncover, increase flame, put ½ tsp oil over the pancake and turn it. Let it cook for 1 minute.
6. Take it out on a plate and spread with jam or honey and roll up.

BREAKFAST

The day should always begin with a good breakfast. The recipes under this heading are all very nutritious and at the same time very filling. As a mother you will feel satisfied to send your child to school and can be assured that he is not hungry before lunch time.

DALIA UPMA

Picture on facing page

Serves 4

1 cup roasted dalia
3/4 cup water
1 tbsp oil
1 tsp rai (mustard seeds)
½" piece ginger - finely chopped
1 small onion - chopped
1 small carrot - chopped
½ capsicum - chopped
1 tbsp green peas
1 potato - chopped
1 floret (a small piece) of cauliflower - chopped
1 tbsp chopped coriander leaves
juice of ½ lemon
salt to taste

1. Soak the dalia in 3/4 cup water for half an hour.
2. Heat oil in a pan. Add mustard seeds, let them splutter for 30 seconds.
3. Add chopped ginger and chopped onion. Stir for 1 minute.
4. Add potato, carrot, peas, capsicum & cauliflower, stir well for a minute.
5. Add salt . Cook covered on low flame till the potatoes get cooked.
6. Drain the water from the dalia and mix with the cooked vegetables. Stir for 3-4 minutes, then add 1½ cups water. Cover to cook on low flame for 2-3 minutes or till water is completely absorbed.
7. Add juice of half lemon and sprinkle coriander leaves on it. Serve hot.

Vegetable Delight

Serves 3

3 slices of bread
2 tbsp atta (wheat flour)
4 tbsp besan (gram flour)
1 small carrot - grated, ¼ cup bottle gourd (ghia) - grated
oil for frying, 1 tsp chopped coriander
½ cup water, ½ tsp salt
a pinch of red chilli powder

1. Mix wheat flour, gram flour, salt & red chilli powder. Add ½ cup water to make a batter of thick pouring consistency.
2. Add grated carrot and ghia.
3. Dip a slice of bread in it and thoroughly coat in the batter on both the sides.
4. Shallow fry in a pan, putting oil on the sides.
5. Turn and fry on both sides till golden brown. Cut into two triangular pieces and serve with tomato ketchup.

VEGETABLE BREAD PIZZA

Serves 4-5

5 slices of bread
3 cubes cheese (60 gm) - grated
1 tbsp cabbage - very finely chopped or grated
1 tbsp carrot - grated
2 tbsp butter
some tomato ketchup

1. Preheat oven at 200°C.
2. Mix together cheese, cabbage and carrot.
3. Butter the slices. Spread the slices on a plate.
4. Spread some of the vegetable-cheese mixture evenly on it.
5. Add a few drops of tomato ketchup on each slice.
6. Grill in the preheated oven at 200°C for 4 minutes or till the cheese just melts.
7. Take out immediately and serve hot.

Snacks

Snacks are the favourite of all children and also adults. But you as a mother would want your child to have less of this and more of the other food. But if the snacks could be made more nutritious, one would not have to say no every time the child asks for them. They are quite easily one of those things which fill those empty moments between main meals.

DELICIOUS ALOO BONDA

Serves 4-5

6 medium potatoes - boiled, peeled & grated or mashed
1 tsp rai (mustard seeds)
1 inch piece ginger - finely chopped
½ tsp haldi
1 tsp salt, or to taste
½ tsp chaat masala
a few curry leaves
1½ cups besan (gram flour)
1½ cups water
½ tsp Eno fruit salt
a pinch of ajwain
oil for frying

1. Heat 1 tbsp oil in a pan. Add rai, let it splutter.
2. Add chopped ginger, fry for 30 seconds and then add the curry leaves.
3. Add the mashed potatoes, haldi, salt and the chaat masala. Mix thoroughly and stir fry on medium flame for 5 minutes. Remove from fire.
4. Spread the potato mix in a big, flat plate and let it cool.
5. Mix besan, water, Eno fruit salt, ajwain, salt to make a thick batter.
6. Heat oil in a kadhai.
7. Make small balls with the potato mixture (the size of a ladoo).
8. Dip it in the thick batter and deep fry.
9. Serve hot with tomato ketchup or green chutney.

Paneer Rolls

Serves 4

200 gms paneer - grated
½ cup coriander - finely chopped
1 cube cheese - grated
1 tbsp maida
1 bread - dipped in water and squeezed
½ tsp jeera powder (ground cumin)
salt to taste
oil for frying

1. Mix all the ingredients except oil.
2. Make small elongated balls and shape them into 1½" - 2" rolls.
3. Deep fry in oil till golden.
4. Remove from heat and serve with chutney.

Macaroni in Tomato Sauce

Serves 2

½ packet (1 cup) uncooked macaroni
1 cup cabbage - finely chopped
1 carrot - finely chopped
2 medium sized onion - cut into thin slices
1" piece ginger - finely chopped
½ cup tomato sauce
½ tsp salt, or to taste, ¼ tsp pepper
3 tbsp oil

1. Add ½ packet macaroni in boiling water to which some salt is added, and boil till macaroni turns soft.
2. Heat oil in a kadhai on high flame. Add the onion, cabbage, carrot and ginger. Saute for 3 minutes. Add salt.

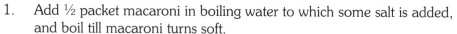

3. Add the boiled macaroni to it.
4. Add the tomato ketchup and mix well. Add pepper and remove from fire. Add more pepper if you find it too sweet.

CREAMY NUTRITIVE NOODLES

Picture on facing page

Serves 2

1 small packet (200 gms) chowmein
¼ tsp black pepper
½ tsp salt, or to taste
2 cubes cheese - grated
4 tbsp cream
1½ tbsp oil
1 medium sized onion - finely chopped
1 medium tomato - finely chopped

1. Heat some water in a saucepan and boil the noodles with ½ tsp of salt. While boiling, add ½ tsp oil to the water to prevent the noodles from sticking together. Cook for 1-2 minutes till just cooked. Do not overcook it. Remove from heat & strain. Rinse thoroughly with cold water. Strain and keep aside in the strainer.

2. While the noodles are cooking, mix cream, salt, pepper and half the cheese together.

3. Put 1½ tbsp oil in a frying pan. Add the chopped onion. Stir fry till light pink.

4. Add the cream mixture and immediately also add the boiled noodles to it.

5. Stir well and cook for about 5 minutes on medium to high flame. Remove from the flame. Serve hot with tomato ketchup.

CHEESY BALLS

Serves 4

1 slice of bread - grind in a mixer to get fresh crumbs
2 potatoes - boiled and mashed
1 tbsp suji (semolina)
1 tbsp nutrinuggets - ground to a powder
2 cubes cheese - grated
¼ tsp salt, ½ tsp jeera powder (ground cumin)
1 tbsp finely chopped coriander
oil for frying

1. Mix all the above ingredients very well. Make small balls.
2. Heat oil in a kadhai and deep fry the balls to a golden colour.
3. Serve hot with tomato ketchup.

Note: *Nutrinugget granules may be ground to a powder in larger quantities and stored in an air tight bottle.*

Nugget Shami Kebabs

Serves 4

1 cup nutrinugget granules - soaked in water for 10 minutes
¼ cup channa dal - soaked in warm water for 30 minutes
1 medium potato - boiled
1" stick dalchini (cinnamon)
¼ tsp jeera (cumin seeds)
1 moti illaichi (black cardamom)
1½ cups water
½ tsp salt, or to taste
½" piece ginger
2 tbsp cornflour
1 tbsp suji
¾ tsp chaat masala
2 slices of bread - soaked in water and squeezed
oil for frying

1. Soak nutrinugget granules in water for 10 minutes and channa dal in warm water for ½ hour. Drain dal.
2. Squeeze out from water from the nuggets. Boil nuggets and dal with 1½ cups water along with whole garam masalas, jeera & salt in a pressure cooker on high flame till one whistle. Reduce flame and let it be on low flame for 5-7 minutes.
3. Cool and grind with a small piece of ginger to a paste.
4. Add cornflour, suji, chat masala, soaked & squeezed bread slices and mashed potato. Mix it all very well and make small kebab like tikkis.
5. Heat oil and deep fry the kebabs till golden brown. Serve hot with chutney.

Corn Vegetable Cutlet

Serves 4

1 full bhutta (corn cob)
2 medium potatoes
100 gm paneer
½ cup cooked rice
2 slices of bread - soaked in water and squeezed
1 tbsp suji
salt to taste
½ cup chopped coriander
1 tsp roasted jeera powder (bhuna jeera powder)
oil for frying

1. Take out the green husk from the cob. The grains should be tender. Break the corn into 2 pieces and boil it in a pressure cooker along with 2 washed potatoes.
2. Remove the corn kernels by scrapping with a knife. Peel the potatoes.
3. Mash together the corn, potatoes, paneer, cooked rice, suji and 2 slices of bread soaked in water & squeezed.
4. Add salt, jeera powder and chopped coriander.
5. Make into small oval or heart shaped cutlets and either shallow fry in a pan or deep fry.

Note: *These cutlets can be served as it is with sauce or chutney or can be put into bread or buns as burgers.*

DAL IDLI

Serves 4

1 tbsp Channa dal
1 tbsp dhuli Moong dal
1 tbsp dhuli Urad dal
1 tbsp saboot Moong
1 tbsp saboot Masoor
1 tbsp rice
1½ tbsp nutrinugget powder - made by grinding nutrinuggets
1 tbsp coriander chopped, 1 tsp ginger - finely chopped
1 tsp Eno fruit salt
salt to taste

1. Soak together all the dals and rice in 3 cups of water for 4-5 hours.
2. Grind the above in a mixer to obtain the consistency of a dosa batter.
3. Add chopped coriander, finely chopped ginger, nutrinugget powder and salt.
4. Keep it aside to ferment in a warm place for at least 8 hours.
5. The mixture should be of medium consistency.
6. Add Eno salt and mix well.
7. Grease an idli mould with some oil and pour the batter in the mould.
8. Boil 1 cup water in the pressure cooker. Place the idli container in it, cover the lid. Do not put the weight. Let the steam come out from the nozzle. Reduce flame and leave it on this flame for exactly 10 minutes.
9. Remove from fire and using a knife's sharp edge, take out the idlis. Serve.

Idli Pakora

Picture on facing page
Serves 4

This can be made using idlis from the market or using idlis made by the instant idli mix available in the market. Idlis can also be prepared fresh at home. The recipe is given below.

IDLI
1 cup dhuli urad dal
1½ cups uncooked rice
¾ cup cooked rice or ½ cup raw poha - soaked

1. Soak the urad dal and rice separately in water, overnight.
2. Grind dal in a mixer. Keep aside. Grind the soaked poha or cooked rice alongwith the soaked rice.
3. Mix both the batters. Add 1 tsp salt. Keep it aside to ferment in a warm place for at least 8 hours.
4. The mixture should be of medium consistency.

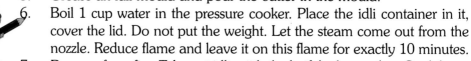

5. Grease an idli mould and pour the batter in the mould.
6. Boil 1 cup water in the pressure cooker. Place the idli container in it, cover the lid. Do not put the weight. Let the steam come out from the nozzle. Reduce flame and leave it on this flame for exactly 10 minutes.
7. Remove from fire. Take out idlis with the knife's sharp edge. Cool them.

FILLING
green chutney or coconut chutney

PAKORA BATTER
¾ cup besan, ½ tsp Eno fruit salt
½ tsp garam masala & red chilli powder
¼ tsp amchoor, ¾ tsp salt

8. For the batter, mix besan with enough water to get a thick pouring batter of coating consistency. Add Eno, salt & spices.
9. Cut each idli horizontally and put a layer of the chutney on one piiece. Cover with the other piece. Dip the idli in batter and deep fry in oil. Cut into two or four and serve.

Nutrient Snacks

Serves 4

1 cup dry nutrinugget chunks
salt & pepper to taste
oil for frying

1. Soak soya chunks in water for 20 minutes.
2. Heat oil in a kadhai.
3. Wash the soya chunks with 2 changes of water.
4. Squeeze the chunks well. Wipe dry on a clean kitchen towel.
5. Deep fry in oil till light brown.
6. Sprinkle salt & pepper and serve.

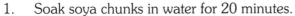

Rice Pakora

Serves 4

1 cup cooked rice
½ cup besan (gram flour)
½ tsp Eno fruit salt
½ tsp salt, or to taste
1 onion - very finely chopped
1 inch piece ginger - very finely chopped
½ cup finely chopped coriander
½ tsp ajwain (carom seeds)
a pinch of hing

1. Add ¼ cup water to the rice and grind it in the mixer.
2. Add all the ingredients to the rice paste. Mix well.
3. Make small rounds on your palm & flatten them.
4. Deep fry them in oil till golden brown on both sides.

Dal Pakora

Serves 4

You may substitute these dals with the ones you have in the house. Use 1 cup of mixed dals in more or less equal quantity.

3 tbsp moong chilka
3 tbsp saboot urad
3 tbsp channa dal
3 tbsp dhuli masoor dal
1" piece ginger, ¼ cup chopped coriander
juice of ½ lemon, ½ tsp ajwain (carom seeds)
salt to taste

1. Soak all dals together for 5-6 hours or overnight, in water just enough to be absorbed.
2. Drain the excess water, if any. Grind it in the mixer with ginger, chopped coriander and salt to a thick paste.
3. Add juice of ½ lemon and ajwain. Make round balls and deep fry.

Savoury Lollipops

Picture on page 69

Makes 8

6 ice cream sticks or wooden spoons
½ cup kale channe - soaked and boiled with just enough water
2 potatoes - boiled
2 slices of bread (preferably brown bread) - crumbled
1 tbsp tomato ketchup
1 tsp salt, ½ tsp garam masala
½ tsp red chilli powder and ¼ tsp amchoor

1. Pressure cook channas till soft. If there is any water left, cook on fire till almost dry. Remove from fire and cool. Grind the channas to a paste.
2. Mix boiled potatoes, bread, ketchup, salt, garam masala, red chilli powder and amchoor to taste.
3. Make balls and insert a stick in each.
4. Flatten the ball on the stick.
5. Shallow fry in a pan till golden along with the stick in hot oil (one at a time).

Sandwiches

Sandwiches are perfect snack food. They can be eaten anytime of the day. They could be carried for picnics in tiffin box or can even be taken for breakfast.

In the next few pages you will find some ideas on how to use fillings in a variety of open and stuffed sandwiches. Each one of them is very nutritious and could be a great treat for your child.

Sandwich Faces

Interesting for a child's B'day party!

Serves 12

6 slices of brown bread, 6 slices of white bread - cut into circles with a biscuit
cutter or a sharp edged lid of a bottle
butter - enough to spread
some finely cut cabbage or lettuce

FILLINGS
2 tbsp poodina chutney
2 tbsp cheese spread

FACES
1 carrot - finely grated (for hair)
¼ capsicum - cut into tiny squares (for eyes)
6 glace cherries - cut into half (for nose)
a firm tomato - cut into small thickish strips (for mouth)

1. Cut two circles from each slice of white and brown bread. Butter all circles. Spread chutney on two brown circles and cover each brown circle with a white circle. Similarly make round sandwiches of white and brown bread with cheese spread. Keep aside.

2. Sprinkle some finely cut lettuce or cabbage on a platter. Place the sandwiches with the white side up, leaving some space in between the two sandwiches.

3. To make faces, arrange a few shreds of **finely** grated carrot on the top $\frac{1}{4}^{th}$ portion of the sandwich rounds to make the hair.

4. Place $\frac{1}{2}$ of a glace cherry to make the nose.

5. Arrange tiny squares of green capsicum for the eyes. Cut a small, semi circled, thickish strip for the mouth.

OPEN GRILLED SANDWICH

Serves 1

1 bread slice
1 tbsp chopped onion
1 tbsp chopped tomato
1 tbsp chopped capsicum
1 cheese slice
1 tsp butter
a pinch of salt and black pepper powder

1. Mix all the chopped vegetables and put salt and black pepper powder.
2. Apply softened butter on a bread slice. Sprinkle vegetables and cover it with a cheese slice.
3. Bake in preheated oven at 200°C for 3-4 minutes or till cheese melts.

Cheese & Cucumber Sandwich

Serves 2

4 slices of buttered bread

FILLING
2 cheese cubes - grated
½ cucumber - finely chopped (¼ cup)
1 tbsp white butter or cream
pinch of pepper

1. Mix all the ingredients of the filling together.
2. Spread in-between the slices. Cut the sides and then cut into two triangles. Serve.

CHEESE-RAISIN SANDWICH

Serves 4

8 slices white or brown bread - lightly buttered
4 tbsp raisins (kishmish) - soaked in water
3 cubes (75 gm) cheese - grated
3 tbsp milk
3 tbsp eggless mayonnaise

1. Soak the raisins in warm water for 5-7 minutes. Drain off.
2. Blend the grated cheese with milk and mayonnaise.
3. Add soaked and properly drained raisins.
4. Butter all the slices lightly. Spread some filling on a slice and cover with another slice.
5. Cut into two and serve.

Note : You may reduce the amount of raisins (kishmish) for adults.

CARROT & APPLE SANDWICH

Serves 2

4 slices of buttered bread

FILLING
1 carrot - grated
2 cubes cheese - grated
¼ of an apple - peeled and grated
a pinch of pepper

1. Mix together grated cheese, carrot, apple and pepper.
2. Spread this mixture onto 4 buttered slices and cut the edges.
3. Cut into triangles and serve.

BREAD UTTAPAM

Serves 2

¼ cup suji (semolina)
5 tbsp malai
2-3 tbsp water
2 tbsp onion - chopped
1 tbsp tomato - chopped
1 tbsp capsicum - chopped
¼ tsp salt
3 tbsp oil for shallow frying

1. Put malai and water in suji. Mix well.
2. Add all the chopped vegetables and salt in the above suji mixture. Mix.
3. Heat a non-stick pan & put 1 tsp oil. Spread the suji mixture on one side of bread & put the plain side on the heated pan. Cook till light brown.
4. Turn the side and pour 1 tsp oil. Cook till the colour of suji changes.
5. Serve hot with tomato sauce.

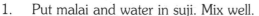

Meal Time Dishes

Meal time dishes are very important because it is during lunch and dinner that the child gets to have the full meal including rice, chappati, vegetables, dal, soup etc. Both vegetable and dal recipes are included under this heading.

Vegetables play an important role in our diet. Properly chosen and eaten, cooked or raw, they make an invaluable contribution towards the supply of vitamins and minerals. Pulses and dals on the other hand are rich sources of vegetable proteins. A good balance of both is essential for proper growth.

NUTRITIOUS ALOO MAKHANA

Picture on back cover
Serves 6

about 15 baby potatoes or 5 medium potatoes - boiled
½ cup roasted peanuts, ½ cup makhana
2 tbsp ghee, 2 tbsp tomato puree
a pinch of hing, 1 medium onion - finely chopped
1 tsp dhania powder, salt to taste

1. Grind the roasted peanuts. In 1 tbsp ghee roast the makhana.
2. Cut potatoes into two if large, or leave whole if using baby potatoes. Shallow fry potatoes in oil on high flame.
3. Heat 1 tbsp ghee in a kadhai, add hing, then add the chopped onion and saute till just light pink. Add dhania powder. Fry for 1 minute.
4. Add the tomato puree and fry for another 1 minute.

5. Add the potatoes, makhana, peanut powder and 2 cups water. Let it blend well and boil till the desired consistency is reached.
6. Add salt to taste. Remove from fire and serve.

CHEESE & POTATO BAKE

Serves 4

3 potatoes - cut into round slices
1 large onion - cut into slices
2 tbsp butter

CHEESE SAUCE
3 tbsp butter
3 tbsp atta (wholw wheat flour)
2½ cups milk
2 cubes cheese
salt, pepper to taste

1. Preheat the oven to 180°C/350°F.
2. Peel the potatoes and slice them finely into rounds. Boil in salted water till just done.
3. Slice the onion finely. Melt 2 tbsp butter in a sauce pan over a low heat and cook the onion on low heat until slightly soft. Remove from fire.
4. Melt 3 tbsp butter. Add atta and stir for 1 minute. Add milk and stir till thick. Add cheese, salt and pepper. Remove from fire.
5. Butter the baking dish and spread a layer of sliced potatoes, using half the potatoes, on the bottom and spread some onions over it.
6. Add a pinch of salt and half of the cheese sauce mixture.
7. Repeat the potato layer, then onion layer, ending with the cheese sauce layer.
8. Put the dish in the preheated oven. Bake for 15-20 minutes.
9. Decorate with a sprig of coriander or parsley. Serve hot.

Red Fried Rice with Soya Nuggets

Picture on back cover
Serves 4

1½ cups (250 gm) uncooked rice
½ cup nutri nuggets - soaked in warm water for 20 minutes and squeezed
4 tbsp oil
2 flakes garlic - crushed & chopped (optional)
1 onion - chopped finely
¼ cup very finely sliced french beans
1 carrot - grated
½ big capsicum - diced
½ cup shredded cabbage
½ tsp of each of salt & pepper
1 tbsp tomato ketchup (according to the colour desired)
1 tsp vinegar (optional)

1. Boil rice and keep aside till absolutely cold.
2. Wash nuggets in several changes of water. Strain, squeeze and keep aside to drain well.
3. Heat oil. Stir fry garlic and onions till onions turn transparent.
4. Add nuggets and stir fry on low heat for 5 minutes.
5. Add beans and stir fry for 2 minutes.
6. Add carrots and cabbage. Stir fry for 1 minute. Add capsicum.
7. Add salt and pepper.
8. Add rice.
9. Add vinegar & tomato sauce.
10. Add salt to taste. Stir fry the rice for 2 minutes. Serve.

CORN CARROT DELIGHT

Serves 4

½ corn cob (fresh)
3 medium carrots - finely chopped into small cubes
200 gms beans - finely chopped
1 large onion - cut into 6 big pieces
1 tsp finely chopped ginger
salt to taste
½ tsp ajwain
1½ tsp tomato ketchup
a pinch of red chilli powder
3 tbsp oil

1. Boil the corn in water in a pressure cooker and cook for 5 minutes on low flame, after the first whistle. Wash with cold water & scrape off the corn kernels with a knife.
2. Heat oil in a kadhai. Add ajwain and let it turn brown.
3. Add the roughly chopped onion. Stir for a minute.
4. Add the beans. After 2 minutes, add the carrot and the corn. Mix well.
5. Cover and cook on medium flame for 3 minutes.
6. Remove lid, add salt & tomato ketchup and the red chilli powder. Mix well and serve hot with parantha or chappati.

Note: *If corn is not available, you may use ½ cup shelled peas instead.*

PALAK LAJAWAAB

Serves 4

½ kg palak leaves (roughly 1 small bundle)
200 gms paneer - grated
1 medium onion - finely chopped
1 inch piece ginger - chopped
4 flakes garlic - chopped
1 tbsp tomato puree
¾ tsp salt, or to taste
a pinch of hing (asafoetida)
1 tbsp ghee
2 tsp almond powder
1 tbsp fresh cream or fresh beaten malai

1. Put the palak leaves with ½ cup water to boil. Boil for 3-4 minutes. Cool. Blend in a mixer to a puree.
2. Heat ghee in a pan. Add hing, chopped ginger & chopped garlic.
3. After 30 seconds, add the finely chopped onion to it. Reduce flame and fry onion till light brown.
4. Add tomato puree. Mix well.
5. Grate the paneer and add to the fried onions. Increase flame. Fry for 2 minutes.
6. Then add the palak paste to it. Cover & cook for 3 minutes on low flame.
7. Add the almond powder and fresh cream. Mix well. Remove from fire. Serve hot with chappati or rice.

Note: *Almonds can be ground and stored in an airtight bottle in a refrigerator for future use.*

CHANNA PALAK

Serves 4

½ kg palak - discard stalks and take only leaves
1 cup kabuli channa - soaked overnight
1 medium onion - finely chopped
1 tsp chopped ginger and 1 tsp chopped garlic
OR
1 tsp ginger-garlic paste
1 medium tomato - chopped finely
1 tsp dhania saboot (coriander seeds)
1 tsp jeera (cumin seeds)
¾ tsp salt, or to taste
2 tbsp oil

1. Soak channas overnight. Boil in a pressure cooker till soft.
2. Wash palak leaves in cold water thoroughly. Put the palak leaves with ½ cup water to boil. Boil for 3-4 minutes. Cool. Blend in a mixer to a puree.
3. Lightly roast saboot dhania and jeera in a clean kadhai. Dry grind to a fine powder.
4. Heat oil in a kadhai. Reduce heat. Add the chopped onion and fry till golden brown on low flame.
5. Add the ginger-garlic and fry for another 2 minutes.
6. Add the chopped tomatoes. Fry for 2 minutes.
7. Add the boiled channas. Mix well. Add the dhania jeera powder. Mix.
8. Add the palak paste and salt. Cover and cook on low flame for 3 minutes. Remove from fire & serve hot.

Palak Soya

Proceed as for palak channa, but instead of boiled channas, add soaked and washed soya nuggets.

Chatpata Masala Soyabean

Picture on facing page
Serves 4

1 cup soyabeans
3/4 cup water
1 large onion
2 medium tomatoes
4 flakes garlic
1 inch piece ginger
½ tsp haldi (turmeric powder)
1 tsp chaat masala
2 tbsp refined oil
salt to taste

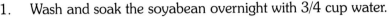

1. Wash and soak the soyabean overnight with 3/4 cup water.
2. Pressure cook for 10 minutes after the first whistle, with 1 cup water.
3. Heat oil. Add finely chopped ginger and garlic. Stir for 2 minutes. Add the onion and saute till light brown.
4. Add the finely chopped tomatoes to this mixture and stir till it leaves the sides of the pan.
5. Add salt, turmeric and the boiled beans and saute for two minutes.
6. Add 1 cup water and simmer for 5-10 minutes.
7. Sprinkle chat masala. Serve hot.

Beans in Coconut

Serves 4

250 gms french beans - stringed and cut into very small pieces (½")
1 inch piece of ginger - chopped finely
1 medium onion - sliced finely lengthwise
½ cup fresh coconut - grated
1 tsp rai (mustard seeds)
3 tbsp oil

1. Heat oil, add mustard seeds and cook till they splutter. Add the ginger and cook for a minute.
2. Add onion. Fry for 2 minutes.
3. Add the chopped beans. Mix well.
4. Add all the coconut except ½ tbsp. Add salt, mix well. Cover and cook on low flame for 13-15 minutes.
5. Remove from heat and sprinkle the left over coconut and serve with paranthas.

BAKED CORN

Serves 4

3 saboot bhutte (corn cobs)
3 cubes cheese - grated
a pinch of salt
a pinch of pepper
2 tbsp finely chopped coriander

WHITE SAUCE
2 tbsp maida
2 tbsp butter
2 cups milk
salt and pepper to taste

1. To make white sauce, heat butter in a kadhai and stir in the flour. Cook for 1 minute on low heat. Do not let it brown. Remove from fire and add the milk gradually, stirring continuously. Mix well. Return to heat and cook, stirring continuously till it turns thick and starts coating the back of the spoon. Add salt and pepper to taste. Keep white sauce aside.
2. Boil the corns in a pressure cooker for 15 minutes on low heat after the first whistle, or till they turn soft.
3. Wash with cold water. Scrape off the corn kernels with a knife.
4. Mix corn kernels with the white sauce. Add 2 cubes of grated cheese.
5. Transfer the above mixture into a baking dish and spread the remaining cheese over it.
6. Bake in a preheated oven at 180°C for 10-15 minutes or till the cheese is brown.
7. Sprinkle some chopped coriander on it and serve hot.

MYSTERIOUS DAL

Serves 4

1 cup arhar dal
1 tomato - chopped, 1½ cups chopped cabbage, 2-3 beans - chopped
¼ cup shelled peas, 1 carrot - chopped

BAGHAR

2 tbsp ghee
½ tsp jeera (cumin seeds), a pinch of hing (asafoetida)

1. Boil together tomato, cabbage, beans, peas, carrot with 1 tbsp water & salt in pressure cooker. Keep it on low flame for 2-3 minutes after the first whistle. When it cools down, churn it in a mixer to get a puree.
2. Strain the puree to remove the skin & seeds.
3. Boil some arhar dal and mix in the above puree.
4. To temper the dal, heat ghee, reduce heat and add hing. Wait for a few seconds. Add jeera. When it turns golden, add to the cooked dal and vegetable mix and serve.

NUTRITIOUS YELLOW DAL

Serves 4

1 tbsp nutrinugget granules - soaked in warm water for 5 minutes
1 cup arhar ki dal
1 tomato - chopped finely, 1" piece ginger - chopped finely
salt to taste

BAGHAR (TEMPERING)
2 tbsp ghee
½ tsp jeera (cumin seeds), ½ onion - finely chopped

1. Soak nutrinuggets in warm water for 5 minutes. Remove from water and squeeze off excess water. Wash thoroughly with cold water.
2. Wash arhar dal and put it in the pressure cooker. Add the above nutrinuggets, chopped tomato, ginger and salt. Add 3 cups water. Pressure cook to give 1 whistle and then keep on low flame for 5 minutes.
3. To temper the dal, heat ghee, add jeera. When it turns golden, add onion. Stir fry till onion turns brown. Add to the cooked dal and serve.

CHEESY CORN SOUP

Serves 4

1 bhutta (corn cob)
1 cube cheese
1 tbsp cream
1 small carrot - chopped, 1 tbsp cabbage - finely chopped
¾ tsp salt or to taste

1. Break the corn into 4 pieces and pressure cook in 5 cups of water for 10 minutes on low heat after the first whistle.
2. Remove the corn and save the liquid. Strain the liquid.
3. Put the above liquid on fire in a container and add salt, finely chopped cabbage and carrot. Let it boil on low heat for 3-4 minutes.
4. Scrape the corn from the cob and blend in the mixer with ½ cup water.
5. Strain it and add to the above boiling liquid. Boil for 2 more minutes.
6. Remove from fire and add the grated cheese and the cream. Serve hot.

CHEESE SOUP

Serves 4

1 tbsp butter
1 large onion - chopped, 1 carrot - finely chopped
2 tsp cornflour
¼ tsp salt, ¼ tsp pepper
1½ cubes grated cheese, 1 tbsp coriander chopped
water or vegetable stock

1. Melt butter. Add carrot & onion. Stir until onion turns soft and just starts to change colour.
2. Stir in the cornflour, gradually add the stock or water and bring to a boil. Add salt and pepper. Cover and simmer for 20 minutes.
3. Liquidise or sieve the soup and return to the pan. Bring it to a boil.
4. Remove from heat and add 1 cube grated cheese and stir. Add finely chopped coriander.
5. Reheat gently and serve in the bowl with the remaining cheese.

Moong & Peas Pulao

Serves 4

¼ cup saboot moong dal - soaked for 3-4 hours
½ cup shelled peas
1 cup basmati rice
1 tbsp ghee
1 small onion - sliced lengthwise
1" piece of ginger - finely chopped
½ tsp jeera (cumin seeds)
½ tbsp butter
½ tsp salt
juice of ½ lemon

1. Cook the rice in an open container with water or pressure cook with 1½ cups water along with the soaked moong so that the grains are separate, with a pinch of salt and lemon juice.
2. Cook peas in salted boiling water for 5 minutes on low flame, covered. Drain it.
3. Heat ghee in a large pan, add the sliced onion and chopped ginger, stirring constantly for 5 minutes.
4. Add the cooked rice and the boiled peas. Stir everything together and cook for 2 minutes.
5. Add butter & mix. Remove from heat and serve hot with curd.

Optional: *Beat 1 egg, make a hollow in the rice, pour in the egg and cook for 2-3 minutes and stir into the rice.*

NUTRITIOUS PAU BHAJI

Serves 4

6 pau (buns)
25 gm butter

BHAJI
1 cup very finely chopped cabbage
1 cup very finely chopped carrot
1 cup very finely chopped beans
1 cup boiled & mashed potato
2 onions - finely chopped
2 cups finely chopped tomatoes
1½ tsp ginger-garlic paste
2 tsp pau bhaji masala
3 tbsp butter
1 tsp salt, or to taste

1. Keep the chopped cabbage, carrot and beans to boil in a pressure cooker with ½ cup water and ½ tsp salt for 2-3 minutes after the first whistle.
2. Heat 2 tbsp butter in a kadhai, add the chopped onion, keep frying on medium flame till pink, then add ginger-garlic paste to it.
3. When the onion turns brown, add the tomatoes and ½ tsp salt and fry well till the tomatoes are very soft.
4. Add the pau bhaji masala & mix thoroughly. Also add the mashed potatoes and mix well.
5. Add all the boiled vegetables along with the water if any. Mix thoroughly and fry till it is of required consistency.
6. Cut each half bun into 2 pieces and spread the bhaji on them and serve.

Cool Drinks & Biscuit Cake

Milk could be one of those things which your child hates to have. But your poor little child does not know that it is very important for his growth. He has to have it without any excuse. So why not give him some variety in this too. He might just love one of these flavours and you would feel so relaxed for his having the milk in this form.

This new cake is a good cross between a cake and a biscuit which can be eaten as a pudding or as a wicked tea time treat. The clever thing about it is that you don't have to bake it in the oven but just put it in the fridge until it sets hard.

Quick Chocolate Biscuit Cake

Picture on page 2
Serves 4

200 gms Marie biscuits (1 large packet), 1 cup chocolate sauce (ready-made)
2½ tbsp cream, 10-15 blanched & chopped almonds, 1 tbsp kishmish (raisins)
¼ cup (10-12) glace cherries - chopped finely

1. Line a cake tin or a small square borosil dish with a large piece of aluminium foil. Press the foil carefully.
2. Break the biscuits into tiny pieces and put it into a shallow pan (paraat). Add most of the cherries, keeping aside some for the top.
3. Add the raisins and almonds to the biscuit mixture.
4. Add cream and chocolate sauce into the biscuit mixture. Mix everything well. Put the mixture into the tin on the foil and level it with a spoon.
5. Press the left over cherries on top. Cover the cake with the foil from all sides and press it down firmly. Put the cake in the fridge for about 2 hours until it has set hard. Lift it out of the tin. Peel off the foil. Serve.

BISCUITY CHOCOLATE SHAKE

Serves 1

6 chocolate flavoured biscuits
1 tbsp honey
1 tbsp vanilla ice cream
1 cup milk
a small milk chocolate, optional, for garnishing

1. Break the biscuits into large pieces.
2. Mix all the ingredients in a blender and blend for 2-3 minutes.
3. Pour into a glass and decorate with grated chocolate.

Honeyed Banana Shake

Serves 1

1 tbsp vanilla ice cream, 1 tbsp honey, 1 cup milk
1 tbsp fresh curd (it should not be sour, if sour do not add curd)
1 banana

1. Peel & slice the banana.
2. Put all the ingredients in a blender and blend for a few minutes.
3. Pour in a glass with straw and decorate with a slice of banana.

Bournvita Shake

Serves 1

2 tbsp bournvita, sugar to taste, 1 glass of milk - chilled

1. Mix bournvita, sugar and milk in a blender. Blend to get a frothy nutritive shake.

$\mathscr{N}ita\ \mathscr{M}ehta's$ BEST SELLERS (Vegetarian)

INDIAN Vegetarian

NEW CHINESE

NEW MICROWAVE

Eggless Desserts

Indian **LOW FAT**

Vegetarian **CURRIES**

QUICK MEALS

More **PANEER**

Dal & Roti

Desserts Puddings

MUGHLAI
Vegetarian Khaana

Green Vegetables